Baqadey

Jeffrey Brathwaite-Izzaak

authorHOUSE

AuthorHouse™
1663 Liberty Drive
Bloomington, IN 47403
www.authorhouse.com
Phone: 1 (800) 839-8640

© 2019 Jeffrey Brathwaite-Izzaak. All rights reserved.

No part of this book may be reproduced, stored in a retrieval system, or transmitted by any means without the written permission of the author.

Published by AuthorHouse 09/11/2019

ISBN: 978-1-7283-2660-3 (sc)
ISBN: 978-1-7283-2659-7 (e)

Print information available on the last page.

Any people depicted in stock imagery provided by Getty Images are models, and such images are being used for illustrative purposes only. Certain stock imagery © Getty Images.

Poetry
A Karriacou Indigenous Art shore-print.

© Jeffrey Brathwaite-Izzaak, 2019

Other collections by the author:

Poetic Duty I
Poetic Duty 1.5
Tears of the Drum

Covers and sketches by Olga Miksche, Bristol, UK
Photo Credits (E. Stiell & G. Cayenne) – CPM in the Mainstream of the Revolution © 1981, Fedon Books
All other photos the property of the author

This book is printed on acid-free paper.

Because of the dynamic nature of the Internet, any web addresses or links contained in this book may have changed since publication and may no longer be valid. The views expressed in this work are solely those of the author and do not necessarily reflect the views of the publisher, and the publisher hereby disclaims any responsibility for them.

On Deck

Bagadere 1
The Shipwright 4
Allert By The Sea 6
Surging Waters (Fries) 8
Virginia By The Sea 10
Friday Evening Millionaires 12
Kayak Assets 14
Dan Ivan 17
Lucy For Darwin 19
Bess 22
Sands Dumfries 24
Andronicus Unmarked 25
Dumfries Oil Discovery 27
Carnival Legacy 29
Island Road (2019) 31
Landeed 33
AWASH 34
    I — Michael Caesar 34
    II — Dorothy 35
    III — Ethan Mark 35
    Overboard. 37
Bogo (ligi) 47
Man Chicko 49
Fallen Star 51
The Day You Gone… 54
Livestrong 61
The Maroon 64

Charge Room...65
Bagadere Revised 67
Lamentation Of A Kayak Seaman................................ 68
Sailing Away 70

Notes 73
About the Author.. 77

Its greem salt kingdom sweeps us out away steep down beyond our power
Beyond the camber of the keel where it's too old for knowledge

The sea is ours- Kamau Brathwaite

"There is an extensive natural harbor, completely land-locked, adjoining Harvey Vale Bay on the south west of the island, which is famous for a delicious oyster found on the mangroves growing in the water."
The Grenada Handbook

Baqadere

I

Enter the gateway
Of mangrove touching tender the everglade corner
To kiss a panorama of stretched water

This inner pasture,
Mermaid's playground
Hidden beaches of gravel and sand
With secrets beyond that beckon you come

Touch here
Search here
Bagadere
Oysters near, pearls sparkle in the wetland meadow

II

By a patch of white sand
Canute chanced upon
A lady fair
Corals of flowing wet hair

Painting him a prophecy
Odyssey from a blue sea
Sparking the obsession
Brush spun upon vivid imagination

Consider this reef of gifts
Dazzling in a game of hide and seek
Imagine Uncle Tommy guarding the gate
Synchronized dance of roots with oyster freight

Enter the village to find the meaning,
Shipwrights caulking decks before launching
Echo of drums, scuttled hulls, new beginnings
From an enclosure not always willing to reveal its origin.

Canute Caliste – 1914-2005

III

Monday, June 6, 1796

Upon the haze of midday
The lookout on Jealous Hill
Saw distant masts appear
Fluttering the Cross of Saint George aloft into the bay

During the heat of anticipation
A force de démonstration
To quell a rebellion
An overnight calm
Before the unleashing of *Fedon's* rainstorm

How could the marines fathom
The secrets of the serene inlet,
Unless its depths were plumbed
And winds whisper the sounds of the land's dialect?

In the respite of midday
Africans congregated by the shore
Conversing in a tongue only they knew
Sharing schemes of flights of return
Gathering dreams to preen wings for the voyage outbound

Abercromby drew his boots upon *Palmiste*' black sand
Gun-holstered, sword drawn
Reverberating a wave of imminent destruction
The previous day's calm long forgotten

In the K of the land
The Karibs and the kribs drowned,
But the mermaid swam
To return on a day of scorching August sun
Sketching portraits to surface in the hand of a 9-year-old

Ralph Abercromby (1734-1801) – General, British army, in transit to Grenada during Julien Fedon's uprising

In 2013

The Shipwright

Man, look like we had to catch wind with *Sails Vanishing* to grudgingly nod we head and say,
'Yes, you *is* a mariner, shipwright of the highest order; first grade even though your modesty wouldn't ride such egotistic water.'
Maybe *Jassie C*, maybe *captain Steele* from L'Esterre; but not simple you on ten toes walking without shoe
In this land of 'Fight Down' you can ask man like Desland
And even if they didn't care whether you did burn or drown;
Look at the difference you make man
On the sailing landscape of this Caribbean!
So when they see you and your pickney in movie
Who could say if is the stem of a tree of jealousy
Make you own yard people wouldn't come and give a hand
In congratulation
To say, 'well done you seaman'

You well salle like them same white cedar ribbing Genesis
and Exodus bow to stern
In retro and introspection we glad that you launched the
life-boat and hold the rope
And was wearing long pants – like some premonition
Not just *Claud*e – 'in the truth' – giving thanks
We who grew up by the sea watching Windward sloops
Glad you still afloat to this day and say,
Man, yeah, yeah, yeah.
Yes man.

'In the truth' - 'residence' of the deceased.

Allert By The Sea

In a moment of sacred solitude
A man alongside the Caribbean stooped
To took a closer look

Behind the veil of history
Memories folding like waves at sea
The sun glides into night, today.

These things seen
Along Neptune's rim – coastlands and horizons
Shipwright, merchant, sailor, owner of seines
Stars, compass, stones of ballast, reefs and wrecks,

When the tongue clips the salted spray
Are the keels rolling on steels of modernity?
Or the rhythm of axe felling sea-grape and mahogany?

On this beach of my ignorance
The sands escape before I understand
The seine line snaps before I pull in the right questions
Our wishes don't last forever
Canute plays the fiddle, then paints the picture
The sound of a drum and triangle iron
Simple rhythms of life-long companions

Pants foot like waves break up
Angel Star under sail rig-up
Watch her sail man!
I hope you find a quiet satisfaction
I yearn to dip a peep
Into your reflection on the beach

EDWIN 'FRIES' STIELL was born in L'Esterre, Carriacou

Surging Waters (Fries)

These waters that made us
Shape us
Tamper our jib and mainsail canvas
Can also bend and break us
Carry and ship us never to come back

Like how we been making a Revolution –
Marching,
Believing,
Saluting;
Non-aligned in solidarity
Swimming in the waters of our own sea
In our own minds
Waves, waves, waves in the backyard of our little pond

Then the sea changed –
Violence in the waves

Waves of blades
Waves of guns
Surging waters –
In which our hopes were drowned
Without return
Swimming in the sea, lost in the ocean

"Like a ship that's tossed and driven
Battered by the angry sea
Say the tide of time was raging
Don't let the fury fall on me"　　I Know – **B. Marley**

Virginia By The Sea

Yesterday, it was the turn of Virginia
To be reunited with her ancestors
Beneath the great silk cotton canopy

And as the echo of gravel on hollow wood ascended
The presiding minister lifted a dirge
And the black and white clad attendees followed

Virginia lay quiet, undisturbed, but for her music in my mind
Posthumous wailings by Marley and Black Uhuru
Stacked with other tracks on the bamboo rack

On the day of her wedding balloons swung from indifferent rafters
I gathered bottles
Drinking the uncertainty questioning the thereafter
But now she says goodbye to all that
And what does it matter?

She had made this journey
JA to the USA to her village – Petite Carenage
That she couldn't see this time

Snagg broke rank to count time in grains of sand –
Facing the lighthouses of the worn peaks of Union Island –
To see but not look in that direction

Yesterday it was her
Tomorrow, us all
Virginia? Yes girl
Wah we go do if the man say so?

But there was no man
Just Virginia covered in deep sleep by the beach.

Friday Evening Millionaires

What you drinking!

Friday evening,
Millionaires on the Esplanade
Arthur Guinness, Dutch Heineken, 6416 and green Stag
from Trinidad

What you drinking?
Start the weekend
Touch bottle heads
Reefer your eyes red
Hold a meds

You mad!
Allen get paid ah few hundred
So now he reach
What you drinking!
Boy ah used to teach start to preach
You don't know is just that some people and money
Can't sleep one night in one house in peace

Millennials before the turn of the century
Out in force spending work money
A different vibes; new feeling
Freedom and rum – new meaning
Baby, if that's something
It means even in Carriacou the world is changing

Friday evening
Millionaires turn paupers
Riches to empty pockets
Going home broken
I got paid today the one token
You high.
I nice.
Good times.
On ice.
Girls passing.
Nuff vice.
That's it.
Friday evening please come again.

Kayak Assets

I

Kayaks have gold
Kayaks have oil
Carriacou have plantations
Cocoa, nutmeg, spice in Jack Iron

Kayaks have it nice
Smoke food and roll rice
So let them pay a higher gas price

Carriacou have 14; Grenada 1
Carriacou have rivers, lakes, mountains an' bush yam
Season growing year round
Poor Grenada have none.

To keep Grenadians alive
Kayaks must subsidize
And pay the higher gas price

Because of bobol,
Kayaks travel the world
Make prime ministers
Them big; Grenada small
Cows, sheep, the Grenadian dove by seven waterfalls

And is Kayak boats
Keep Grenadian traffickers afloat
So give them a different quote

They preach it
We accept
Grenadians love it
Roads, schools, stadium
Desalination plants, new port, new supermarket!

Store shelves clean down
After Ivan
Ice in pan, everything we send down
'Boy, they so nice!'
They really mean Kayaks dumb.

They too independent and resilient
Carriacou always give and Grenadians always want

II

Gas gone up
Bus fare up
Dolly C arrive in port
What the Revolution stop just come back
Royal GPF conducting stop and search

They practicing apartheid
Black on black man
Flagrant, biased, jealousy ride
Penalize and treat we like a bad sore
Why citizens not free to walk ashore

Gas gone up
Grenville and Hillsborough same stock
We pay more
We more black

But this blatant segregation
Been going on since long ago days
Grenadians won't change?
Ask for black wine, Heineken, whisky and brandy
We go send everything
Because Kayaks full ah money

Gas gone up
Salary stuck
Ivan bring ice
Emily wasn't nice

But why the victimization?
Kayaks fed up
Collect you jerry cans
And ride on jackass back!

Who keeping quiet
Is it a plot?
What going to happen
When donkey stop work?

We getting less while paying more
But most Grenadians only hear about Carriacou
So why they treating us so?

Dan Ivan

This was a beating of brutal proportions
It was terrible; it was Ivan

After one, Kim roof gone
Bathsheba silent
Galvanize sail like a windjammer
Curse words done

From early ah dig a drain
Was more wind than rain
But it couldn't contain
Clothes in barrel start swimming

Roof peeling like sardine tin
Galvanize wrap round branch and stem
Tornadoes climbing up mountain
Not Texas, not Wyoming
Mt. St. John, right beside Tan Ine ole kitchen

It was dread
Wind blow, me heart shred
One time when ah take ah peep
Botha from Grenada was walking the street

Every time ah say it done
The wind raise up ah new storm
Me brother was on the phone
All lines wet, Ivan change the ringtone

Badang bang!
Like the roof time come
Water coming down
5 pm, no end to Ivan

Ah did check the dog
Move the pig to higher ground
Nobody remember the girl Lily
Ivan, was the dan

Lucy For Darwin

Dear Darwin,

Please don't find it inane
But permit me to ask something.

Ah know Lucy, her black origin
The long journey across the African horn
But what I can't understand (hence my question)
How did Lucy get ah man?

It's ah great leap from a fish in de sea
To apes swinging in de trees
A woman naked on the beach
To a million people on the streets of Guangdong
If she began all alone
Where did all the children come from?
This procreation is my confusion
If Lucy was the beginning
And every egg needs a sperm
Then where did Lucy's donor come from?

This is not the egg and the chicken
Then ten hens scattered in the yard by one cock on the run
Monkey and ape to me
Appear in the same state to be
So what's going on?
I don't fathom the intricacies of natural selection
And my life too short to comprehend years in a thousand

Much more a million billion
Neanderthal intermediary
Naturally, have you ever known primates to mate with humans?
Was Lucy all alone in the Rift Valley?
Or was she hiding in the garden with Adam?

How did she know she should procreate?
To make humans
Who get so smart
They put the world in a sad state
And racism is so absurd
They degrade their originator
Making primate sounds, throwing banana skins
Blaspheming their god
If they resort to calling us apes
Either Lucy had a man
Or the whole theory is fake

Darwin my friend,
I'm not planning a trip to the Galapagos
I don't feel like watching iguanas and tortoise
So as the man who observed the finches
And responsible for the evolution
The new truth
In school, church, and on every radio station
The new religion

If Lucy was in Africa
And now her children spread all over
And is the only way we know it to happen
Then we assume is so it began

So how long was she alone?
And,
Way de hell
Did she get a man from?

GORDON CAYENNE was born in Mount Pleasant, 1947, educ

Bess

You know,
We don't want to write another elegy
Inked with afterthoughts of apology
Brethrens speak things clearly,
But man can't bring news to the Almighty

So we write ah line on dis time
To say
The way you influence plenty minds
Youths dreaming visions
Above the village grass-line

Science of agriculture – *Carinut* – new approach
Down to earth, bolts and nuts,
Study and bring back a share of knowledge by facts

How else in the world
We woulda get word about *Conference of the Birds*?
Some people talk when some people shouldn't say a word

And you know we not adding up sums
Just passing the history forward a generation
Who scratched a mark in the soil of our ground,
Even though, Jah know, Gordon Cayenne.

Sands Dumfries

Uriel Joseph

The sands of conversation
Making of islands
When friends steep in warm waters
Tumbling their stuff in the surf and
Fluff of the early morning
Raising skeletons of driftwood, boulders and mangrove
Reflecting on ancestors, freedom,
Sacrifices year-go-year-come
And our flight – flight of return
Yemonja, an entire ocean
Between us and the Yoruba coastlands
Streams of shipwrecks, wells, lakes and rivers
Because these services in the chapel of our days
Clear as the rolling waves mixed with suspended grains
Shall not revisit us often again as brethrens
So let us soak our lives in these mornings
When we return to sacrifice our thoughts on this shore…

Andronicus Unmarked

How could twenty years pass-over
Without an epilogue to his letter?
The diggers broke the unflinching rock,
The minister proclaimed his ashes to dust

A firstborn who lost his daddy
Dropped-out of school early
But pursued the scholarly
And shared notes with Garvey and Gairy

*'Permit the expression of my opinion,
We must better insure the land heritage of succeeding generations.'*

Now, like the kings of Arabia
In death a man needs nor gains stature
Except remnants lodged in memory
Still, how surprising to see

No memorial to mark the spot
But a mound of diminished earth
How Jos and Paulina must now mourn
No mark was written for their beloved son

Andronicus Jacobs served as Senator for Carriacou and Petite Martinique in the late 1960's. He was also a member of Marcus Garvey's United Negro Improvement Association (UNIA), while living in the USA.

Dumfries by D Sea

Dumfries Oil Discovery

Just as Stalin foretold
Carriacou strike gold
Oil dump in Dumfries
Green and plenty like seaweed

Camoon and Sabazan witness the lottery
Horoscope gamble like Play Whe
New employment
Oil luxury sweet like honey

They never thought that Carriacou could have this thing near a lagoon by the sea
They thought was just lime tree, melon, the dump, Skylark, Engine and Rasta Frankie
But is continental shelf running deep from Siberia to Belle Vue.

New land, new contrasts,
Moscow will pay for that
Start the party
Wet fete, shorts and bikini

Bulldoze the cemetery
Not even the dead could stand in the way
Bring tanker, build jetty,
If you think you seeing jumbie
Is the oil money making dummy

Oil for the people
Russia to the rescue
Rich deposits off-shore
Natural gas win like jackpot bingo

Is not a dream
Check the scene
From the beach Dave and Peters still sand mining
Gazprom survey the fields
Rich yields to pump
Then we'll build an airport for the tycoons and oligarchs to land private jets beside Dumfries dump

On the way to J'Ouvert

Carnival Legacy

Big legs, thin legs, yes legs, more legs
Sandal-strapped gladiators on the march
Cleopatra, Nefertiti,
Loaded, side, front and back
Heavy bone, solid fat

Whole legs, pure legs
Smooth and tough tan
See legs, go legs,
Carnival revelation, asphalt fashion

Beausejour and Caco
Milan, New York, London, Tokyo

Fair legs, bleached legs, dark and lovely brown
One life, more life, legs get it on
Cannes brulé – burn cane, free the Africans

Slavery done!
Expression of a naked freedom
See Eve walking her way to Adam

Carnival and legs
Ole-oil and skin confrontation
Legacy of explosion
Legs got it on!

Belle Vue main road, 2019

Island Road (2019)

And finally,
After *Gairy, Blaize, GNP, Revo, Primo, Nimo,*
Sylvester, Patterson,
Toby and Mt. Royal men walking shoes in hand
Sense behind back in jola sack,
Donkey, mule, Nick board bus and government truck

Finally, after Albert done turn fifty three
And cousin Celina in Brunswick cemetery now 4 years nearly
Robertson didn't live to see
Neither *Teh Teh*
Cousin Mitch after all the years breaking boulders in Dumfries quarry
Cousin Herbert dig he grave, season he rum, now he lay down and gone, in the truth and not again,

And finally,

After so many floating jetty
Kuwaiti fund, *World Bank*, *OECS* and *CCC*
Independence, constitution 74 and 1973
Campaign to plant a tree in Belle Vue
Cedars fell to keel boats in Windward and L'Esterre
Shut down, turn round, *Barbs*, *Nixon*, *Bernard*, *Rodney*
Red, Yellow, Green
And 45 years in Laca Pierre
Piece by piece
If ants coulda carry the news…

Call *Lincoln McIntosh* in England
Tell him the island finally get a little attention
Call the Dead the Bury the Disappeared
Cousin Jim, *Tehvah*, the *Lendores* and *Wilsons*
And who hear tell the others if you here
You know it look like Belle Vue road go finally done (this year)?

Landeed

The wall wasn't enough
So we built an outside fence
To claim what's Ours
From henceforth hence

The gap wasn't enough
So we ran chains across
To claim what's Ours
And prevent trespass

The gate wasn't enough
So we put up a sign
'Private property – keep off!'
'If it was yours then, now it's mine!'

God's world wasn't good enough
So man built up his kingdoms
Borders, the earth crisscrossed by
Wire, concrete, steel rods and stones.

The dust is not enough
So we build concrete tombs
To claim what is Ours
For eternal rest every man needs his private room

Awash

I

Michael Caesar

The sea is our river
Parting islands

The tide our ruler
Measuring distance

From time
Our gold mine

Natural extension
How far we've been
How near we've come
Pools in which we swam

The sea remains our river
Our everything

Our ocean
In which we swim

II

Dorothy

Grand Mal harbour sweeps your hair astern

Long-liners
Long nighters
Pelicans, trawlers and tankers anchored at sundown

A slanted sliver of bronze illumination
Quickly slides and divides the bay

On the hill,
The verandah waits remodeled
The jupa mourns in shutters
In darkness quiet the schooner slips its berth
With gravity a *julie* falls from its mango perch.

III

Ethan Mark

He paced the sterile corridor
Of the ward
With the rod of his contempt

That God would
Consign him to the scrap yard
Before he could convert or repent

This fire burned
Silence to his lips
Visitors spurned by the heat of his ferment

I paced my anger through days of disbelief
'Not Ethan of all men!'
I could not reconcile the bitter taste of the treatment

Overboard.

In the twilight
Where ships raise the land
And the spirits of sailors turn home
To the welcome of hearts adrift
And arms that reach for a seaman's gifts
From the world where they exist

A seaman! A sea man! What is a seaman?
Married, eleven children, at sea since the day I was born. The sea stands in my blood. The sea, my world, rolling all around. The sea is my backyard, my home. Dripping in my veins. The sea salt season every strand of my thin mane; seeping through my pores.

I built boats – row, sloops, a schooner. I caulked hulls – wick and tar seaming vessel creases by mallet hammer. I sailed the Caribbean, fished the hues of blues around the cays and islands. Off British Guiana, these hands pulled snapper from brown water. I spent more time on the sea than on land. The sea wraps me in destiny – no me without the sea, no sea without me! I live *by* the sea, *in* the sea.

I love my family. I care for my family.
Tonight, this beautiful moonlit night, I have decided – finally.

Wednesday 28th, March 1973.
The Wife:

I bore him eleven children.

My husband and four sons built a fishing and cargo boat 39 feet long, called Marie-Anne. It was beautiful, painted white with a green stripe. It is what we call locally, a sloop – a sailing sloop – no motor. He used to say, "My lady Marie run the waves as a gazelle – that girl beautiful like hell." It used to make me smile.

My husband was the owner and captain. They often sailed up North, St.Barths and as far south through the Trinidad Bocas.

Most of the time, any one of my sons would accompany their father. Other men from the village would also sail on trips with him. Many of these sailors however, would not stay long – one or two trips and they would quit, as they had families, and sailing did not guarantee a reliable income.

Thursday 29th March 1973
Sailor One:

I am a married man. I live with my wife and children.

I am related to the captain. I have known him for most of my life.

He owns the fishing vessel Marie-Anne, and I work with him on the vessel.

On Saturday morning at about 10 am, I left the village in company with the captain and one other sailor.

Thursday 29th March, 1973
Sailor Two:

I am 32 years old. I am a single man living with my mother and father.

On Saturday at about 10 am, I joined the captain with another sailor from the village to go fishing. We sailed in the boat that belongs to the captain and his wife. We were going on an exciting voyage and I was very excited about it… We were going fishing around the islands to the north.

The Captain:

I married young. It is the village custom. Marry, children, hard work, make me-self a man. And, if they didn't turn out good-for-nothings, they would remember to return the favour to their old man.

Ah Marie-Anne! Eleven is a heavy burden to carry, 9 months at a time baby. Nine times eleven is ninety nine! One more and we would hit a century!

The wife:

My husband left home on Saturday morning in the company of two sailors from the village.

Both men are related to my husband, and generally speaking they are very good friends. They usually visit us at home. This was the second trip for one of them. The other is a regular – he has sailed with him many times before.

At about 9 am my husband left home saying that he was going to fish. When he left, he did not mention any particular spot or area. He often speaks about banks – snapper, butter fish, hind banks. I imagine they would go fishing on one of the banks.

As far as I know, my husband left with about ten to eleven dollars in cash. He had a few drinks before he left; but I can tell that he was not drunk that morning. I do not know if he took along any liquor with him when he was leaving, neither do I know whether there was any onboard his vessel.

Sailor One:

Money?
What you say?
Who say?
I had no knowledge or any idea about monies in the possession of the captain. I did not see him with any money. He did not tell us he had any money. Our trip was to catch fish to sell to make money to look after our family. If the captain had enough money then I don't see why he would be going to sea to get money. Penny in hand better than a penny in sea-bottom.

Sailor Two:

Money? The captain never told me he had money on the ship and I don't know if he had money.

The Captain:

Marie-Anne my beloved. I think about the children you gave me; although you say is me give you them. Is true what the old people say, 'You make children, but children make their [own] mind.'
But when you accuse me Marie!
Me! Marie! Marie Me?

I swear!
How you could think that way of me! My own flesh and blood!
That son of mine, say he building boat too. But is money he studying. Money make he mind. He like money. Anyway…

I stand up here in the island moonlight. No shadow in my night. The bag is empty Marie. Just me flashlight for this extra journey. Compass set already. Wind is calm; I see the lighthouse … set my course, sailing steady.

The Wife:

Whenever my husband is drunk he usually suffers from some sort of nerve trouble. As if he going off his head, saying all sorts of things.
A few months ago he was taken to the doctor at the hospital for the said complaint. From thence he was undergoing treatment from the doctor. The doctor advised him to stop drinking many times; but he did not stop.

30th March 1973
The Doctor:

I am in charge of all the medical activities on the island for the past two years and eight months.
In the course of my duties as medical officer the Captain was under my medical care. He had more than one attack of Paranoia for which he was treated at hospital as an inpatient. The last occasion was in late December, during which time I advised his wife not to allow her husband to go on sea-trips

because his mental condition was a potential liability to those in his company and himself.

Against my advice, the wife took her husband from the hospital at her own discretion.

The Wife:

Sometime a few years ago, while he was sailing on a ship called Abiding Star, it was daytime and the nerve trouble occurred and he jumped overboard, but he was rescued by the other men on board.

On another occasion, he went to the police station asking the police to lock him up. He was then taken to the doctor for medical attention.

The Captain:

'Mental.' People have it to say how I crazy.
Paranoid? I don't know what de doctor mean.
A man like me with 11 children can't be crazy. I find I had me mind all the time. Me mind never leave me. I built this ship, sailed this ship, fish in this ship. I didn't build it from paper; I build it from my head. My head not sick, but sometimes I does get ah little weak. I have a drink to steady me nerves. Make me sure on my feet.

I have decided. *My mind's made up and I won't turn back.* Thank you Lord Jesus! Maybe I too could walk on sea as you did on Galilee. Amen.

Sailor One:

While we were fishing near the islands between Sunday night and Monday morning, something happened. I don't know what it was, but we heard the captain talking saying a lot of awful things. The three of us was on the deck of the vessel. Then I and the other sailor told him to go and lie down in the cabin.

He replied, 'I am not going and lie down,' and, 'don't study me.'

We told him again, 'Go and lie down and rub your head with some limacol.'

He then said to us, 'I told you all don't study me, leave me alone.'

Sailor Two:

When the captain came on deck he was wearing a blue pants, a blue jacket and a grey felt hat, no shoes. He had a bag slung over his right shoulder.

The Wife:

They say it was Sunday after midnight. Monday morning, one o'clock. He was on deck. Took his flashlight. Looked at his watch. Don't know what was on his mind, maybe he was checking the time. Seamen always checking the time. They read the sun, moon and stars – the planets. They know the skies. My husband knows how to tell time by these things. Nothing else I can imagine.

Sailor One:

The three of us was on deck. I was steering. The other sailor was in the bow. The captain was standing near the cabin. He was talking to himself and laughing. Is not unusual for him to talk and laugh to himself. I do that too, but what he was saying wasn't like usual talk. Is like he had lots of things on his mind. That is why we told him to go rest himself. Instead he say, "It is now one o'clock, time to do my work."

Sailor Two:

The captain left from where he was standing and walked to the stern of the boat.

The Captain:

Peace. Perfect. Perfect peace. I'm walking light on my flight. Ready to do my work. Ready for my journey. All my years on the sea. My destiny. When it calls me, I cannot turn away. Cannot run away. Not now anyway. Not after all it's done for me. My family. My Marie.
I love my family.
When I'm on the waters, I feel at home. On my skin, in my bones. By myself, but never alone. Lee tide, spring tide, high tide, slack tide; water heavy like the full moon. I feel like being born. Born again. Reborn. Life baptism.

Marie-Anne was christened on a Sunday morning. Father Harry walked on deck, in his white tunic, holy water splashing the planks. Then we bathe her with bottles of Black and White whisky, and *Jack Iron* smuggled from up

North. And when she finally hit the water and float, she was ready for her work.
I'm ready. One o'clock. Time to do my work…

Sailor Two:

Suddenly he stopped talking and threw himself into the sea.

The Wife:

They said that they searched for him up till about 3:00 am the said morning.

Sailor One:

We both then searched up to 3 am and there was no trace of him.

Sailor Two:

We lowered the sails and launched the small boat that was on deck. I entered the boat with a lantern and began searching in the vicinity. We searched the waters until around 3:00 am on Monday the 19th, but did not find him.

The Wife:

When they saw that they could not find him, they hoisted sail and came back to the village. Up to this day, there is no trace of his body.

The Captain:

No trace of me? My body? Really?
I'm a seaman. I belong to the sea. My Marie, they say, that's the way some things were meant to be, and some things are not easy to bear.

>They say I took the plunge,
>Disappeared without a trace
>Into the deep without a sound
>Silent like a sinking stone
>I walked ahead straight
>Without regret
>The wind in my face
>Just when her bow kissed the sea
>Parting her lips gently
>The salted spray whispered to me
>'You're a seaman'
>'You belong in this ocean'
>Surrounding these islands
>Believe me
>Evidently
>I am there
>Into the light
>Into the night
>Marie,
>There was no better way.

In memory of the mariners lost at sea

Before Jouvay

Boqo (liqi)

Steve,
You head was big
Taking more than a regular swig
But all them man from Top Hill grieve
That day you done take you bag and leave

You used to call me name
But not again
We know is so it go
When time come, man don't trod the road anymore
Like *Lion, Errol, Crucial* and *Jericho* *

And …
Copee get a stroke we.

He say, "I know is de Almighty smite me."
For when he was playing crazy
And breaking shop all in Grand Bay
Edwin wasn't easy
Going to jail regularly
Even cousin Joycee couldn't get away
De boy hands did sticky

But I don't want to say is juss so it go
As you know
Rum, ganja and cocaine
Dem three,
Could destroy anybody
And so too, bad company

Because when he was in London South East
He used to rave all in Bristol, Liverpool and Man City,
He and dem McLeod boys dem
So dem did stay
Is ah good ting is Carriacou you know
And cousin Polly nevah send you away

So if Copee feel he paying fuh he deeds
Is nuh me wah say
Is juss so it go
And Bogoligi, you nuh day to see
And some man don't believe in R.I.P.
* d. Crucial; Errol. d. Aug, 2019

Man Chicko

Ghosts of lightning prongs burn the morning
Ashes of Armageddon
Thunderclaps, cloud-storm,
Winds snap, waves foam in celestial commotion

Grey rain, signals swim,
Around a sandbar
Pew a cathedral of friends
In the pale waters of the Grenadines

As the beach retreats, I grapple with speech,
Verses tossed by currents against the seabed of my reefs,
Emotions drip tears of grief
Strained through the pain of pure Violet

Walls of the old fort remain
Braced by ancient cannons
Overlooking the town, guarding claims
The hearse appears; how can I explain?

We make judgments as if superior, somehow better men
When only in experience on the battleground of living
We would know who is who:
Who would breakdown
Who would hold ground like the guns of iron
And you stood as the earth shook
Erect
As the boat rocked

Trembling, facing death,
Swirling swells threatening to wash your quarterdeck
Wounded deep
But not cowered
Tossed beyond *Tarleton*
Down *Lopital Sound*
But your faith stood un-lowered
And that is man.

Not house and land
Not money in the bank
Not water tank.

Hold it up Dada
Try not to falter
Through this hurricane the storm must calm
When we wash ashore together on *'Lange Zey Bon.'*

Fallen Star

They say you was a star
Shining among constellations
How you woulda reach far
Near the sun and its regions

They claim to be your friend
Another fallen soldier
How you time was short
45 only
And to get call home
Or somewhere by the master
How them can't understand
But he must ha have a plan
And anyway, he always know better

I ent say nothin'
Just hold my silence
While thinking
Man time coming soon
You ready?
You prepare, like you daddy?
You hope to be aware
Before, eh?

They say
Take you check up
Doh play man;
Every year boy

Know how and way you stan'
This not going to doctor
Until dead ready to come
Antiquated, outdated, macho-ism

They say
We'll be there to take care of the family
You always had a smile
Ah good word
They remember you sincerely – dearly
You leave us with plenty memory
You wasn't political – really
And anyway
That is life
We all make mistakes – many
What's the price?
For talking bad – not a penny
Rest in peace – plenty

They wonder if is genes
If you did feel ah pain
Saw it coming; any inkling
I saw you working
Building your dream
Don't have to claim no connection or anything
Death has no value
So I wish everything was everything

Like how we dey normal
Going through the daily routine
Boops!
Ting get interrupt

And then we go back to living again

People say ting they never tell you face to face
But is not bad mind
They just didn't find the space
Hard to express
And is so we stay yes
Pretentiousness

I am speaking to me as if to you
I wouldn't call your name
Everybody doing the same
Genuine – and some for fame in the worldwide domain

But look, frankly,
People like me shouldn't have much to say
Leave such tings for you family
Talk or not, all ah we ending up right dey

So me boy,
Remember we used to joke about the belly
We was never thinking that we woulda separate so early in the play
You hear me?

The Day You Gone...

I
It don't matter when you choose to die
Whether Sunday is better than another day
Or if is hot sun, rain, overcast, lightning or storm.

You have nothing to gain
Than to inconvenience people and their plans.
And too besides,
Is not you who decide
And don't be like 'Ghaddafi'
Walk down below tree to confide in a suicide.

And the man say
'Is God that give and taketh away...'

Ah tell you,
And Jeffrey too,
If you thinking
Something go happen to mark your exit
Like a sign, to say you meant something to the keeping of the universe
And something, someone, somewhere, take notice
And so it go rain on the day of the funeral
Flood, like never before
Or clouds do something people never see
Because you is some pillar missing...

Is that same vain feeling you entertain
How the plane go crash
And you go be the only one surviving…

And the man say,
'Is two choices'
Heaven
Or yeah,
The rich man and Lazarus parable.

Anything could happen man
When is time to call you to go
You don't have to put things away
And fix up you self to get ready
Is dead you dead, regardless.
[But you want to look nice!]

II
And ah did tell you
But let me tell you

You see dat girl
The one you used
To make stupit with
Talking about how you love…
Guess what?
She cry,
Two weeks after she gone Grenada
And meet the fella
She did liking before you.

That is why ah was telling you
Dead, and you go see

And them woman
All them woman you say is yours
With your seeds and waters scattered all over the estate
Because you is some stud
The best ting before sliced bread

You remember ah
Tell you me mother say,
'Watch that John
He think he could kill it
[Stupid man] but dead he go dead and leave it.'

When they see for true is you in the coffin
They shake their head:"Oh gud do doo!"
Me mother! Me belly!
But same way
Their life continue
You didn't kill it for true.

Them people in work come out
They give speech
They take picture
They really feel it
They say
Not a man
In the world like you
Like so again
You get ah good turn out

And you remember
How you used to think
Is only you alone
Way could do the work
And the work can't work without you…
Like is you way make the work
And made for the work
You ent taking holiday
You ent going far…
[You have to be there… near]

Remember?
Yeah man
Since you gone
Work stop – done
In fact, more than th'at
World done.
Ah tell you
You was the man
Even the President
Call to say
He couldn't come

They raise you flag that day!
Raise you nose
Me boy
They give you ah good send away
You woulda proud

A, A
And the boy…
The one with you and the land nuh

He didn't laugh
He just remember
How you was getting on wid him
'You didn't know is dead you go dead so'
But he ent rejoicing
He was just talking
All he saying,
"Watch him now
Way he dey now?"
Boy wha you woulda do if you was watching in truth?

That is why ah tell you
Dead
Just play stupid
And you go see

Even them people
How you used to call them?
"Them?"
Well them
Yes all ah them come in happy hour
And you de hate the name too
Well they come
Nobody call them
But is death
They come to sympathize
To show they face drink you rum and fraternize

And the door
You used to keep locked dey
They open that
People walk in the door me boy

When ah see that
Me mind make up
Ah say me boy
It really look like you not coming back …

But was only joke ah was making
When ah say,
'Dead and you go see who coming.'

Ah tell you
"Take a cruise."
"No."
"Make ah child."
"Nah!"
"The money in the bank…"
"Nah- can't touch dat."
You eating crix
Like Lionel
Cheap, cheap
Well,
They buy you a casket
Bury you in a suit
I don't know what's the benefit
Shoes?
No, barefoot
And no socks

When ah see it
Ah check me self
Ah say
Not me again living so vain
Running behind people

Getting hot, hot, over politics
Like that tot
Asking me about what to do
About house and heart
Ah see better now
Is ah good ting you dead
For me to know

Ah used to say
Try ah ting
But like you get serious
Before ah could say
Man, was joke ah did making

Ah want us to live together
Like bredren
Ah wish you could come back
For me to tell you
All that happen since you gone.

Livestrong

Livestrong!
Livelong!
Liveforever!
My confession as a sinner
Selfish bully
Believe you me
It didn't really cross my mind;
Baby I gat the fire
Just like air in your rear tyre,
Bottle of water,
I know,
Insufficient to have a shower…

But I love you
Same way

Yes,
No,
But what's new
That you don't know?
In this world of lights and afterglow
Rights and heights
Hypocrisy the line
Separating wrong from right
We are all on the tow

Can I go to sleep at night?
Can I ever end saying sorry?
But I must say
I love you baby

But I too am no less
A believer
Fierce, faith, dedication
I too would get the reward
10 thousand virgins, milk and honey
Streets of Gold
Riding in my chariot
Let the crowd rise!
The gladiator enters!

For what it's worth
What can I now say?
I do so love you baby

Testosterone belongs
In a man's scrotum
Mountains in my life
King of the climb
Tour de Force
In the saddle
Your everyday champion!

They've won
In bringing me down
The most sophisticated
Sophistication
I love you before

And after
Every blood transfusion
Livestrong!
I Am Strong!
My confession.

The Maroon

There was a maroon again
As its been -
Not by *Tan Dora Junction* -
The drums were laid at the entrance to the school yard
By the *Corn House*.
Some tourists came
Took pictures
But then again,
I asked Joyce,
Granddaughter of a Maroon Queen,
'What's the origin of this thing?'
'What is its meaning?'
And it's like the whole weight of forgotten history fell on me
We never ask questions
Or not the right ones
So I went to the maroon
Kept my shutters on
Because, it's like, I had been to the maroon so many times around
And I needed a new angle
Other than, 'this is our tradition'
'It's what the *old heads* hand down.'
So?
I went to the maroon,
With gaps in my understanding of its function

Charge Room

Hillsborough

Let's begin with your name
Your age – how many years
Way you staying – you single or married?

Excuse me, you spell me name wrong
Well is what you say we put down.

… any children?
Who you living with?
The house – with what material you build it?
Upstairs and down?
Give us the paint pattern and description

Officer, somebody bounce the car
Where it was parked
What kind of question is that?
When we go reach the license registration part?
Just ah minute
We ent reach dey yet
Forever we been doing this
The law is perfect

Not stupit!
The is bull…hit
Don't say it!
What about the car – and it's particular

If it was at home
I wouldn't come to town!

This charge room
Echoes of Westminster, Raj and Delhi
Empire – who we are
And who we think we be
How far we've come and not nearly
I come for help
Like they want to arrest me
And the criminals
Hit and run way ahready.

Baqadere Revised

The mermaid rebound
From the depths of the sound
In the voice of a language not spoken

We scratched shapes on the sands
Surfaced names of the dead beyond
In search of the pure pronunciation

Sunday, next, the schooner sails for Saint Dominque…
'Weep for me …whoever loves me, lament for me…'

And in that lament her eyes glazed
As if the lifting of the haze
To submerge the years of damage

In a song to comfort lonely souls
To stash their pain and grief
Hidden in marshes of relief

If the Africans freed by death
Were to revisit this cove where secrets slept
Maybe they would not recognize the bay
Maybe they would just turn their backs and fly away

Lamentation Of A Kayak Seaman

This one is a dedication to man like Winston and John
And by far they are not the only ones
Aspects of life
Some Carraicouan tradition
Auxiliary schooners on a wind to St.Barths
Sailing down
Through the Serpents Mouth all night long
Barrels rolling in the surf
Up a beach rimmed by sand
To bless counters
Measured shots of Jack Iron
In liquid tribute to those now gone

And when the contents were emptied and the oak casks split
Daniel Akins and Sugar Adams
Drums would shape with the mallet
So tribes and clans
Could find their solace, find their nations, find their feet
Bitter with the sweet, joy and grief
Masts in place – we won't accept defeat

And now the channels have dried
Laws enacted without feelings
Our trade has died
All the long line of sailors
Captains who made us who we are

Brought to nothing
Uncle P, Dada, Uncle C, Cheesy, Gairy, Beckwith, Cold Beers, Philmore
And Canute's sidekick *Sonnel*
Plus the scores I don't know
Who sailed to and fro…

Well, I write in tribute and tears
For that which they've done to the ancient ways
Our traditions unspun
What the ignorant and arrogant have done!

And yet
You are still with me
The way I feel
About you and our history
I bless you with lines
I bless you every time
In the light; in the dark
A little knowledge
But I bless you still
As pioneers who climbed the hill
To taste the sea breeze
And saw ahead and beyond

So take one with me fellas
Leh we remember who we are
Remember until

Sailing Away

Aft

Things fall apart when the elders depart
So we beg, 'stay with us, don't cut us short'
Wisdom we need, words from the heart
We have no beginning, when we have no start

This ground in hollow where they lay us deep
You tomorrow, today, our tears we weep
The memorials are lost, the history shaken
We bear the cost as the flock takes flight – feathers broken

Things fall apart in the invasion
We've got no worth, where is our station?
Shipwrights with cedar, ancient fisherman
We do give thanks for your daughter, the beautiful librarian.

So as we lay you below this earth with the springs thrust open
We sip memories of libations as a token
To soften our paths; our hearts lighten
So that when our ships sail
Jib and mainsail would catch the wind
Rudder tilt and ropes tighten

So even if things fall apart around us
The centres would hold

Keel may age, stern crippled
But our green hearts never fold
We've sailed these waters
Hot and cold
Sail forever
Deep in our soul

Notes

'Bagadere' (noun. C'cou): – (aka Kanash/Great Carenage –Harvey Vale); mangrove inlet; sandy shoal therein; a secret stash-away

Canute Caliste explained the beginning of his artistic gift after a boy - hood encounter with a mermaid

Carinut – Agricultural Co-op Est. c. 1984; now dormant

CCC – Consolidated Contractors Company

Conference of the Birds – By Persian Sufi Poet Farid ud-Din Attar

Corn House (Mt. Pleasant) – House of stone; [historically] used for grain storage

GNP – Grenada National Party (1954/5-1984). Led by Herbert Blaize for most of its existence.

Hold a meds – Meditation

Island Road – Names of politicians, parliamentarians, road contractors and well known villagers

Jack Iron - Over-proof rum popular in Carriacou

Kayak Assets – Since Independence (1973), two Kayaks served as Prime Minister of Grenada: Herbert Blaize (Mt.D'Or) 1984-1989 and Nicholas Brathwaite (Sir) (Mt.Pleasant) 1990-1994. Nicholas Brathwaite also served as Chairman of the Advisory Council after the US invasion (1983) and advisor to PM Herbert Blaize.

'Lange Zey Bon' – Place name, Grand Bay

Lopital Sound – Area of deep, Grand Bay lagoon

Lincoln McIntosh – Island Advocate

Ole heads – 'Griots'/ seniors in society knowledgeable of the traditions

OECS – Organization of Eastern Caribbean States

Up North – Islands north of Carriacou, particularly those with trading links such as Sint.Maarteen and St.Barths

Paga.dey (patios) – 'Do not look!'

Play Whe – A numbers game introduced to Trinidad by Chinese immigrants; now popular in Grenada.

Sails Vanishing – Inference to docu-film Vanishing Sails (2015) by Alexis Andrews

Tan Dora Junction – Traditional site of Mt.Pleasant & Grand Bay village maroon

The Revo – Grenada Revolution, 1979-1983

The Shipwright (event alluded) – Burning/sinking of the MV City of St.George

Uncle P, Dada, Uncle C, Cheesy, Gairy, Beckwith, Cold Beers, captain Philmore and Canute's sidekick Sonnel – Some Kayak mariners/ captains/ shipwrights/boat owners

Yemonja – Yoruba water goddess

In harbours of our lives where our vessels careen broadside

About the Author

Jeffrey Izzaak was born in Newland, Carriacou. Writing since childhood, he studied and performed poetry as a companion of Grenadian poet and playwright Michael DeGale, and a member of the Theatre of Unique Music and Dramatic Arts (TUMDA) collective.
This is his 4th collection.

CPSIA information can be obtained
at www.ICGtesting.com
Printed in the USA
LVHW090903191120
672055LV00024B/552